Set design by Christine Jones

Photo by Carol Rosegg

A scene from the New York production of *Rain Dance.*

RAIN DANCE

BY LANFORD WILSON

★

DRAMATISTS
PLAY SERVICE
INC.

RAIN DANCE
Copyright © 2005, Lanford Wilson

All Rights Reserved

SPECIAL NOTE

Originally produced by the Purple Rose Theatre Company
Jeff Daniels, Executive Director
Guy Sanville, Artistic Director
Alan Ribant, Managing Director

New York premiere originally produced by
Signature Theatre Company, New York City
James Houghton, Founding Artistic Director

RAIN DANCE was originally commissioned, developed and produced by the Purple Rose Theatre Company (Jeff Daniels, Executive Director; Guy Sanville, Artistic Director; Alan Ribant, Managing Director) in Chelsea, Michigan. It received its world premiere at the Purple Rose Theatre on January 19, 2001. It was directed by Guy Sanville; the set design was by Vincent Mountain; the costume design was by Rebecca Ann Valentino; the lighting design was by Dana White; the sound design was by Suzi Regan; the properties design was by Danna Segrest; and the stage managers were Anthony Caselli and Julie Dougherty. The cast was as follows:

HANK .... Matt Letscher
TONY .... Billy Merasty
IRENE .... Suzi Regan
PETER .... Paul Hopper

RAIN DANCE was sponsored by a generous gift from THE MOSAIC FOUNDATION of Rita & Peter Heydon based in Ann Arbor.

RAIN DANCE was originally produced in New York City by the Signature Theatre Company as the final show of the 2002–2003 Lanford Wilson season, opening on May 20, 2003. It was directed by Guy Sanville; the costume design was by Daryl A. Stone; the lighting design was by James Vermeulen; and the sound design was by Kurt Kellenberger. The cast was as follows:

HANK .... James Van Der Beek
TONY .... Randolph Mantooth
IRENE .... Suzanne Regan
PETER .... Harris Yulin

CHARACTERS

HANK
TONY
IRENE
PETER

SETTING

We are at the Cantina in Los Alamos, NM.
A red sunset just now.

RAIN DANCE

HANK. This is the hour that the mountains were named. You can imagine the explorers camping down by the creek — that they called the "Great River." The sun had just gone off everything except the mountains, they're reddish anyway, some, and if there's enough dust in the air to make a really good, red sunset — you can just imagine the priests looking up at the mountains, red as they are now, dropping their shovels or whatever, grabbing their crosses, and saying, "Oh! Bless us! The blood of Christ!" They probably took it as some kind of sign. Why not the smile on Queen Isabella's lips? What would that be? In Spanish? Well, everything was religion with those boys. They were priests, of course, everything was. That was their — reference. Why did the soldiers, explorers, whatever they were, have to drag a priest along on those expeditions? What? Were they botanists or naturalists? Maybe they were expected to convert the "heathen." Neutralize him. Or find the elixir of love or perpetual youth in some new mineral or — (I don't know) cactus. It was just a religious culture, priests were like their chaplains, probably. They — went along. You wonder how the soldiers, or explorers, conquerors tolerated them. "Oh, God, there they go again, with the blood of Christ." Priests. Boy. I don't know. Monks. God, I feel like some kind of monk myself up here half the time. Believe me, it's no wonder they had hallucinations. What's the Indian name for them?
TONY. The priests? I wouldn't want to tell you.
HANK. The mountains, Tony. What did the Indians call them?
TONY. Sangre de Cristos. Like everybody else.
HANK. Sure. I know you have your secret names for everything. That you can only say in your kivas and can't tell the white man. Aren't they sacred? The mountains, I mean, aren't they sacred?
TONY. Oh, sure, but what isn't? The stand of trees by the fork in the river is sacred, the river is sacred, the fork in the river is sacred, the land on the other side of the road, the mariposa lilies. Everything is sacred to the Indians. It's enough to make you sick.

HANK. *(Looking at his watch.)* Okay, Ryan is now officially late.

TONY. Ryan's picking you up?

HANK. Yeah, me and Peter.

TONY. Where's Peter?

HANK. I don't know, but Ryan is now officially late. I've spent my entire year here waiting for that guy. Damn, I hate waiting. God! This place. This countryside. I love it here. I'm more relaxed here than any place I've ever been.

TONY. You're nervous as a guinea hen tonight, you're driving me nuts.

HANK. Tony, for me, this is relaxed, believe me. For tonight. Well, maybe I'm not so relaxed tonight. Who would be. But you can't help but feel the pull of this place, this country.

TONY. More than any place you've ever been. And you've never been any place.

HANK. It's true. Or not like you. Mainly here and the Bronx. Drove up into Canada once. I keep thinking you and the Indians at the pueblo know all the answers. You're just not telling. We've been up here scrambling for the secret insides of things, if we have our answer, which we probably don't, I keep thinking it's going to be something you guys have known all along.

TONY. You talk such bullshit sometimes.

HANK. I knew you'd say that. I wish I could sit like you do; you've hardly moved a muscle in half an hour. I don't know how you do it.

TONY. After the abuse I've laid on myself, when you find a position where nothing hurts ...

HANK. Is that philosophy?

TONY. That's dancing five shows a day and drinking too much alcohol. And living like a fool.

HANK. Sure. You talk in enigmas, Tony. We're on to you. There's at least two meanings and an implied question in everything you say.

TONY. Oh, you drive me crazy. See? You're making me move. The Indian can't hold all the mystery you kids pour into them. They're simple-living people. And poor. You can't understand them so you make them wonderful.

HANK. You kidding? Their whole way of life staggers me; humbles me. You always say "them," not "us."

TONY. Well, see, you can think you've learned something about me.

HANK. Would you have been a chief? If you'd stayed at the pueblo?

TONY. If I'd been a chief I'd have been a very bad, restless chief. Making everyone anxious. It was never a question, I was like you,

6

I couldn't sit in one place.

HANK. You still dance better than any of them. All the older men do, but especially you.

TONY. It's not how good you are.

HANK. I know.

TONY. And it's not for show.

HANK. I know. *(Irene enters.)*

IRENE. Good. You're here. Is it just us?

HANK. Ryan's driving Peter and me. We don't have to be there 'til after midnight. He's late of course.

IRENE. He's always late.

HANK. Well, he's late again.

TONY. That they "called" the Great River? You don't think it's grand? Probably the only river they'd seen in a year? Maybe the only water? You'd have called it the Rio Grande too.

HANK. Oh, but Tony, when you've heard of it all your life, movies named for the Rio Grande! And songs. The border demarcation between Mexico and Texas. The Rio Grande! Come on. You don't expect something twelve feet wide and so shallow you can wade across it without getting your shins wet.

TONY. Well, it's your fault for expecting so much.

HANK. Have you noticed it's always my fault when I argue with him? It probably has good fishing, I'll give it that.

TONY. I wouldn't know, I eat hamburger.

HANK. I have never seen you eat a hamburger once.

TONY. Maybe they discovered it down in Texas, where it's more impressive. And Queen Isabella was a goner by the time the Spanish saw the Sangres.

IRENE. What are you two…?

TONY. Oh, Hank was being wispy and washy again. Dreaming about how the Spanish named the mountains.

HANK. You tell me. What do the Indians call them? The Sangres?

IRENE. I don't know.

TONY. She never learned Tewa. She thinks the Indians should have their privacy.

HANK. Really? You've been here all this time …

TONY. Oh, don't make something wonderful out of it!

HANK. You must think I'm the most naive and gawky kid on the planet. It's almost fun.

IRENE. No, we know how important you are.

HANK. I didn't mean that. Come on.

IRENE. Oppie said you were one of his keys.

HANK. What do you mean?

IRENE. You know how circumspect he is: He said you made a "fundamental contribution." And you wrote a book.

HANK. I wrote a pamphlet. On testing the strength of metals, tensile strength, for architects. Definitely not a big seller. But "wispy and washy," you're right. When it comes to this place, the pueblo, the Indians — they — astonish me.

TONY. You don't know what you're talking about.

HANK. I know. Thanks for telling me.

TONY. Four hundred Indians at the pueblo and the people at the South Square don't speak to the people at the North Square. You think —

HANK. Come on, I'm a wreck here. *(He notices a smudge that's been left on a table and picks it up.)* Whose smudge?

TONY. I don't know.

HANK. Is it really cleansing?

IRENE. Very much so.

TONY. Oh yeah.

HANK. I may have to steal it. Take it back to the Bronx with me. God knows the Bronx needs cleansing. Where's Peter?

IRENE. Up at the lodge. They all are. They were too … loud. It's …

TONY. You know Irene and crowds.

IRENE. There's also that.

HANK. What an amazing team. I can't believe I've been working with them. Peter, all the rest of them. You must have known them all for years.

IRENE. No. Hans, Rabi. Bohr. Fermi.

HANK. I talk to Fermi in Italian, he answers in American slang. The only Italian I've heard from him is opera.

IRENE. You are probably the least Italian-looking man I've ever known.

HANK. I know. Milano. Up north. Half the population is light. Well, a lot.

TONY. More than you'd expect.

HANK. I was only there once, when I was little, we visited some relatives. No memory at all. The folks go into raptures over the place.

TONY. More industrial than most of Italy.

HANK. It probably won't even be there by the time I get a chance to see it.

TONY. The food's lighter.

HANK. Yeah, they're very snobbish about it.

TONY. "Hank"? What kind of Italian name is Hank?

HANK. What? Oh, you knew that. Yeah. Declension: Enrico, Henry, Hank. Like Caruso.

TONY. Only don't sing for us.

HANK. What?

TONY. Where is your mind tonight?

HANK. I'm sorry, Tony. No, I won't sing for you.

IRENE. "Enrico." They couldn't have two of you here.

HANK. Oh, my God, I could never be confused with Fermi. God, what a genius. What a master! Probably you can't tell just in ordinary conversation.

IRENE. No, he gave me a lesson in growing tomatoes. Seed he brought over from San Marzano.

HANK. I know, he gave me a package of seeds I sent to Mom. It killed me that I couldn't say, "Oh, my God, Mom, these are from Enrico Fermi!" God I love that man. Well, admire. Admire that man. They couldn't have done anything — he's all of it as far as I'm concerned. He drives you crazy, of course. He has to have his experiments. Test everything, make models. Patience of Job. All the rest of them are too cerebral for him. But he makes these incredible leaps in logic that just astonish you. No, I've been Hank since kindergarten. I've always been Hank. Second-generation Italians, Americanize everything. My folks call me Hank. They don't know what they are. No, I'm no Enrico. But tomorrow ... Where is that guy? Tomorrow you'll hear, maybe, what all those guys that you know as just yacking quacks —

TONY. Hank.

HANK. — what they did.

TONY. Enough.

HANK. or failed to do.

IRENE. *(She rises to go pour herself a sherry. This is said only to break the tension.)* Nobody ever offers me a drink anymore, why is that, I wonder? That's a rhetorical question.

HANK. I know.

IRENE. I should stop. It's undoubtedly eroding some vital organ or — my brain or kidneys or pancreas or — if anyone knew what the pancreas does.

HANK. Makes digestive secretions, helps digestion.

IRENE. I thought that was the liver.

HANK. They sort of work in tandem. Makes insulin.

9

IRENE. I thought the islets of Langerhorn —
HANK. "Hans" —
IRENE. "Hans" made insulin.
HANK. And they're in the pancreas.
IRENE. Sweetbreads, right?
HANK. I'm afraid so.
IRENE. I love sweetbreads, but I don't think I really needed to know the actual function of the things.
TONY. You don't ask a question on the Hill unless you really want an answer. 'Cause somebody is gonna know.
IRENE. Everything is so classified I'm surprised it hasn't broken me of the habit.
HANK. You actually think about giving up the hooch?
IRENE. I can be very serious about it in the morning. When I went back to the house last month I didn't have a single drink for the whole week. Never thought about it. But laying off "the hooch" is just not the easiest thing for me to do. At least not up here, on the Hill, in this …
HANK. … Godforsaken place.
IRENE. You have that right. He saw us coming and He must have just turned His back in disgust … or disappointment … or sorrow.
TONY. I'd as soon you guys not talk about the work, okay? Whatever it is, He made it possible.
HANK. Oh, but, Tony.
TONY. I'm not playing around here.
HANK. I know. *(Suddenly.)* It's gone. The light's gone. The sun went behind a cloud or something.
TONY. The sun went down. They're still the Sangre de Cristos Mountains whether the light's on them or not.
HANK. This country. God, I love it here.
TONY. Only the second time tonight.
IRENE. The place must be slipping.
HANK. I envy you so much, living here. Being such a part of the place.
TONY. That's the first time tonight for that one. He says the mountains are red because there's dust in the air.
IRENE. Okay.
TONY. And he feels like a monk up here.
IRENE. Oh poor baby.
TONY. I thought that little problem had taken care of itself.
HANK. What?

10

TONY. Haven't you availed yourself of our girls' new service?

HANK. Dormitory Seventeen? You know about that?

TONY. Of course I'd know, it's my job to know.

HANK. Isn't that amazing? I had no idea. It's not my style, really, as it turns out.

IRENE. What?

HANK. Nothing. Nothing.

TONY. With all the single young men up here ... some of the girls in one of the dormitories have a little business going. A little commercial enterprise ...

IRENE. Oh, my God. Of course they do. You have got to admire American initiative.

TONY. Top dollar. Seven bucks a pop.

IRENE. Good for them. Spread the wealth.

HANK. I understand it's a veritable cornucopia: Indian girls, Spanish girls, white girls, that Chinese girl from Oppie's office.

IRENE. Oh, you gotta love 'em. Are there men?

HANK. You kidding me? The time I went by — just to check, okay? — they were lined up. Soldiers, some of the carpenters, the bachelors from S.E.D., pencil pushers.

IRENE. I didn't mean as customers. Do they have men on the menu?

HANK. What? No. God. Of course not. What are you talking — men don't sell themselves like that. *(Tony and Irene are laughing at his naiveté.)* You're kidding me.

IRENE. You are really a dear.

TONY. Anyway, after all the scandal — first the committee decided firing every girl in the dorm was the only way to handle it. But the guys in the bachelor dorms raised such a stink, they were afraid they'd lose some of their best men. So now it looks like they're just going to pretend they don't see it. You like hearing you engineers are human.

HANK. Oh, very. I think we have some frailties that are singular to us.

IRENE. Quite a few. But not our Hank?

HANK. I'm making no promises at all, Irene. It's been a very enlightening revelation for any number of us. *(Hank whispers something in Tony's ear.)*

TONY. You never had anybody do that to you before?

HANK. Tony!

IRENE. He's pulling your leg, Tony. I don't believe it for a minute.

HANK. Well, anyway, I don't have time for it.

TONY. Everybody's got time for a little —

HANK. — Well, then, I don't feel comfortable about it. Like that. My idea is you have to earn lovemaking. You know, you sit in the picture show and you inch your arm around her shoulder, intimacy is something you should earn — you know, one — button at a time. You don't just go in some strange girl's bedroom and drop your pants.

IRENE. Relax, Hank.

HANK. I know.

TONY. You're almost finished up here, aren't you?

HANK. *(This stops him for a moment. Beat.)* We're all looking crazy, huh? Anticipating — whatever. Yeah, I guess. It's getting pretty critical. Triumph or disaster. Well, disaster in any case, but triumph or failure. I'm not leaving New Mexico tonight or anything. Well, hey, maybe tomorrow for all I know. We might all pack up. It's weird. I have no idea where I'll be next week. Maybe back teaching. I can't bear the thought of leaving here. Not Los Alamos, I'll willingly leave Los Alamos, but Santa Fe, the pueblo, Maria and the rest of the potters, watching them work; especially her. The mountains and hills, colors, quiet. You and Peter. Just the expanse of the place. The vistas from the mountains, looking down on the Rio Grande, with those — what are the silver leafed trees with the white trunks, growing all along the river?

TONY. Come on.

IRENE. Hank.

HANK. I thought maybe you'd know.

TONY. What do you think they are?

IRENE. What would they be?

TONY. Los Alamos? They're "the poplars, the cottonwoods." Los Alamos.

HANK. Los Alamos. "The cottonwoods." For godsake. I've been here over a year and never bothered to ask what "Los Alamos" means. This — Has there ever been such a place? Where men come home to wives less than a hundred yards away, and the wives and family have no idea what the men have been doing all day.

TONY. That sounds pretty standard to me.

HANK. No, really. What the explosions in the valley were all about? What … They're wonderful. They don't ask questions. Or I don't suppose they do.

IRENE. I honestly think most of them have no clue. I wish I knew at least less than I know.

HANK. It's so counter to all our natures. Secrecy; all this security. Scientists talk, that's what they do. They talk to each other, they talk among themselves. They talk to themselves. I mean we're absurd loners. We're the kids who retreated to the basement with our chemistry sets. But half the fun, half the inspiration, comes from batting things around. And with these guys — the giants in their — I've learned more just talking to Peter than in seven years of study. It's … God, you've all had such astonishing lives. The greatest minds of their generation. Running, being chased from country to country. Under cover. It's always like that. Every generation, the great thinkers are rejected, persecuted, their books are burned in giant bonfires with gleeful idiots dancing around — it's absolutely Biblical.

IRENE. Hank.

HANK. I know. I think I'm actually shaking. *(He looks at his hand, which is still.)* Well, inside, I'm trembling. You and Peter have always worked together?

IRENE. No. I'm really only an artist —

HANK. — Only an artist —

IRENE. — but Peter had to draw a screw, he couldn't begin to get it right. I don't know how the other wives stand it, playing bridge, dancing the polka, having babies and — have you ever seen so many babies?

TONY. Well, what did they expect?

HANK. I've never understood why the wives couldn't know.

IRENE. You're kidding. A woman? Imagine trusting one of those to keep a confidence.

HANK. We're not that bad, are we?

IRENE. On the other hand, I honestly don't know the specific use of a single thing I've drafted. But to have something to do has been a lifesaver, believe me. "Here. Here is your drawing for the thingamabudgit, whatever the deuce it does."

HANK. I envy you so much, living here all these years.

TONY. That's two. Right?

IRENE. I'm not going back to the house 'til we can stay there. It's too painful having to leave.

HANK. Where's your house again?

IRENE. A hill, just on the other side of the pueblo. The men from San Ildefonso built the house. They let Peter and me help mix the adobe, but they wouldn't let us go near laying the bricks.

HANK. When was that?

IRENE. We've lived there fourteen years now.

HANK. I didn't know you were Peter's wife the first time I saw you. I thought what in the world is a woman like her doing here? Now I can't imagine the place without you. Like you'd always been here. Like the pueblos or mountains or something.

IRENE. Awk! It isn't anything we'd planned, believe me. It was supposed to be just a rest, to get away from the cities and the noise, and with any luck blow the smell of Europe off our clothes. We'd only been in this country five months.

HANK. You must have been a baby.

IRENE. We'd been married just a year.

HANK. I'm sorry, but — what I meant to say was — the first time I saw you — I heard in town that the Indians at the pueblo were doing the — some dance. The one at dawn, middle of January, with the deer coming down out of the woods.

IRENE. Yes.

TONY. Ceremonial Buffalo Dance.

HANK. Buffalo? Really? All I remember are the deer. The men had been holed up in the kiva all night, preparing for it, doing whatever you do. *(A pause. He looks to Tony — nothing.)* Anyway — I couldn't sleep. I hadn't slept since I'd come here. A bunch of us had passes to go watch if we wanted to. I could hear the drums and the singing, middle of the night, so I went over to see it. I think I was the last person to spot the dancers. They come out of the woods so slowly, and move so slowly. You can't tell that they're moving at all. They're almost invisible. They really do move exactly like deer. And it was hardly light. And I was freezing. You were across the way with the Indian women from the pueblo. And you were so like them, except of course for the way you dress and look. But your, I don't know, your soul was …

IRENE. Oh, please.

HANK. I said to Ryan, "Look at that woman over there. She's so still and at peace with herself." And he said, "That's Dr. Snyders' wife." I knew Peter was married and had lived in New Mexico for years, but I thought Ryan was talking about one of the Indian women. I mean, you're so much …

IRENE. Younger? Peter's so brilliant and was so virile and strong. I was swept completely off my feet … And he was swept completely off his feet. There was nothing but air under us.

HANK. Ryan said the Indians had literally adopted you into their tribe. I decided you had been abandoned as a child and raised by the Indians. A foundling.

IRENE. I was raised by the Indians. I was a very late foundling.

14

HANK. I came by day before yesterday for a minute. Peter said you were out. And the day before. No, I know. You get your moods. But, you know, it was cold last night.

IRENE. I took a blanket, Hank. I don't run off crazy. Well, maybe it's crazy, but I've learned to live with it. Sometimes it just all gets to be too much. All right, I know.

HANK. There's nothing for miles except jackrabbits and snakes and the Indians at San Ildefonso, who must be the gentlest people on earth, and they're two miles away. Except for the Cantina when no one's going to be here, you work at your bungalow, you never go to any of the functions.

IRENE. I certainly do. Have. Some.

HANK. Peter never opens his mouth, Tony never moves, and it's all too much for you.

IRENE. Deer and jackrabbits and four hundred soldiers guarding the place and barbed wire fences and three hundred physicists. Excuse me, I mean "engineers," I keep forgetting there are no "physicists" or "chemists" here. All these geniuses you love so much aren't that easy to put up with. Look at you.

HANK. Well, not tonight. Tonight's a completely different —

IRENE. All the milling and going and arguments — I have to go up in the hills and gather myself. This is not why I came here. Well, okay, laugh, you should, I'm ridiculous.

HANK. I was just imagining what you must have been like in Germany. Or New York.

IRENE. We weren't in New York that long.

HANK. No, really, the cities, and the noise and —

IRENE. An absurd, nervous Nelly who was afraid of her own voice, which sounds like me now, but that was a different woman, girl, in Germany.

HANK. Would you go back?

IRENE. Lord no. Can you imagine? All that green would suffocate me. In the south, around Munich it's very lush. All those great masses of green things. I wouldn't be able to breathe.

TONY. She gets asthmatic thinking about it.

IRENE. I do, I'll be wheezing at you, don't talk about it.

HANK. Where did you live?

IRENE. I'm not joking.

HANK. Fine, it's okay. *(He goes off by the door, looking out. Slams the doorjamb with his palm.)* Damn. Where is he?

IRENE. *(After a pause — as a concession.)* Peter's family had an enormous house, in the middle of a park — which I thought was lovely, but now I'd choke. Really.

HANK. I thought you taught school.

IRENE. I beg your pardon. Work? Certainly not. Peter's family would never stand for it. Well, actually I would have liked to. Teach drawing or painting. It isn't for me, I'm not a teacher.

HANK. Me too.

IRENE. Don't be modest. I'm sure you're good. You just look like a teacher.

HANK. I know. No. I'm okay. I'm very calm teaching. You wouldn't know me. It's an act. I stand beside my desk, never sit. It's all very deliberate, very calculated. Huh. I'm twenty-seven and my life is over. This has been the apogee, swinging way out here, so far away from anything in my life before, I'll never see anything like it again. The work. None of us will.

IRENE. You don't ever know that. Look at Tony. Where he's been. Or me. Even Peter.

TONY. You're twenty-seven?

HANK. I know, I look older. I've aged ten years here. Twenty-seven years old, I'm already losing my goddamn hair. Excuse me.

TONY. You make up for it by acting younger.

HANK. How old did you say you were when you came here? I'm sorry, you don't ask a lady her age.

IRENE. I was nineteen. My life hadn't started. I doubted I'd ever have one.

HANK. Yeah, I'm done with the main work. My part. You know, you get afraid that — scientists are early achievers. Even the great ones. Even your friend.

IRENE. We've made so many friends here.

HANK. We all know you're partial to Dr. Bohr. I think we're jealous. No, of anyone else, you can't be jealous of Bohr. He's the gentleman among us.

IRENE. I did enjoy my walks with Dr. Bohr. I wish he was still coming here. He's what Maria called a walkie-talkie, walker and talker.

HANK. I can't imagine either one of you talking.

IRENE. Maybe we just walked. He told me how yeast works.

HANK. Voluntarily? That's a new one. He's so damn diffident you wish he would volunteer more.

IRENE. I asked. I didn't know what I was getting into.

HANK. A lecture on bread?

IRENE. Bread, beer, organic chemistry. I followed it to the extent that the yeast makes bubbles of carbon dioxide that cause the bread to rise. But then he worked out a formula for each meter of rise in sea level which he found the fascinating part but he lost me completely. He also told me what alcohol does to the liver which I could have done without.

HANK. You knew him before here?

IRENE. Peter's known him forever.

HANK. He got out of here quick enough, didn't he? He saw what it was gonna be and got on his horse. It's very dry stuff. Teaching math. It must be exactly the opposite of art. Very factual, very concrete. And pretty opaque. At least to the layman.

IRENE. I'm sure there's magic in it when you know what you're doing.

HANK. Oh! You have no idea. Numbers are heaven. I think they literally may be. The logarithms are our catechisms. But only, I'm afraid, if you're interested in numbers. But it's philosophy, it's music. I used to love the abstraction, it's astonishing to find there's an application for all that geometry. That's great, no I mean it, that you understand there's magic in it, most people don't. I sound like a complete ass, forgive me.

IRENE. I'm afraid I'm most people.

HANK. Never. I'd kept thinking I wasn't really needed here anymore. You're right, Tony, we're almost done. I've been expecting any day they're going to say, "Okay, kid, get lost, you've done your bit." I wanted it and didn't want it.

TONY. I'd as soon you not talk about it, Hank.

HANK. Oh for crying out loud, Tony, not tonight. If you know I work in metals. Mathematics. Theoretical physics. And what the hell does it matter? Not after tonight. We've either got it or not. *(A long pause. There is an adjustment, all three of them realizing they all know what they're talking about.)*

IRENE. *(Musing distantly.)* Everyone's leaving, going to "the site." Whatever that means.

HANK. Ground Zero. I don't know where it is. Probably Tony does.

IRENE. This whole weekend. Starting Thursday night. Actually early Friday.

HANK. — The thirteenth.

IRENE. — Just after midnight. I was up in the hills above the place. A whole convoy, cars and two of the biggest army trucks I've ever seen, moving so slowly they must have been carrying — what? And then more cars and jeeps and trucks all day Friday, all day today.

HANK. I know.

IRENE. Rose Bethe *(Pronounced "Beta.")* couldn't sleep either. She was sitting on her porch. She said, *"Vas auch immer —— ""*Whatever they were moving so carefully last night, I hope they're moving it a long way away."

HANK. Two hundred fifty miles at least, I heard. I don't even know what direction. Ryan knows the road.

TONY. To the middle of nowhere, of course. At least they think so.

HANK. I know. This last week's been twenty-four hour days, it's been exhausting. I can't believe I'm sitting down. One emergency after another. We're improvising. We're filing down these totally unexpected bubbles on nickel plating. Filing with a file so fine you can hardly tell you're working. And smoothing the gaps with gold foil — nothing's too good, right? Filing the foil, just barely touching it. This isn't my field, practical application. Measure, sand. Measure, sand. I'm a theorist, so I'm not used to it. Doing this incredibly exacting — I was literally shaking ... As much from being physically exhausted as real nerves probably, or conscience or trying to grasp the ... and it's hotter than the hinges of hell in there — we're all in shorts and undershirts — dripping sweat ... I had to sleep, I'd been up three days running. I just fell into bed as I was on top of the covers. The sun woke me up. All my clothes and skin, my hands and arms, legs, sandals, the whole bed around me was just, dazzling with these microscopic flecks of gold — just brilliant. Literally glittering ... But ... It's good, it's worked out well. At least we hope.

TONY. Yeah. We're proud of all you eggheads.

HANK. Yeah, how about that? It's good to be used. Be of use. It's been good. We're proud too, I guess. And right on schedule. I think my priest would call that vanity.

TONY. Naw, naw. Hubris, maybe. *(Hank laughs, then begins to cry softly and can't stop.)*

IRENE. It's all right, Hank. It's all right.

HANK. *(A real question.)* Is it? No, I know. I'm sorry. Damn. What time is it?

TONY. Ten-thirty.

HANK. Less than six hours. No, it's not been good. This last bit anyway. To get my work done, most of it, all the math. Having nothing to do. Watching everybody else working, doing my checking, double-checking, fine-tuning. There's too much time to think. Which is definitely not good. Then suddenly one emergency after

18

another, after I'd thought it was over. Ad-libbing. Well, I said. After all the careful … *(Peter enters.)*

IRENE. Hello, darling.

HANK. Oh, great, you would come in just as I'm having a nervous breakdown.

PETER. Don't let me interfere.

HANK. Was that thunder? Tell me that was thunder.

PETER. Yes, they say we're in for a storm. We can't get an accurate prognostication until later tonight. *(Hank steps outside.)*

IRENE. We were just talking about you. Had enough party?

PETER. It's no party. It's nerves. But yes, I've had enough. It's the same old arguments up there. Kist asked me something, I showed him on the blackboard, I'm chalk from my eyebrows to my socks.

IRENE. Why don't you go home and have a quick shower.

PETER. I refuse to call that absurd "bungalow" they have us in "home." I would love to go home and soak in the tub all night, with the hot water running. But I think I'll reserve the experience of our dribbly shower in that ill-lit closet until I've repaired some of my sanity. *(Irene has poured him a glass of sherry.)* Thank you darling.

HANK. *(Reentering.)* It's still in the distance. The sky's gorgeous. Amazing. Mom wrote to me, said with the blackout there are thousands of stars over New York City. Twenty-five years, I never saw one.

TONY. I better go pretend like I'm working.

IRENE. I thought you were off duty tonight.

TONY. I am.

PETER. Don't let me —

TONY. No, I've been on my way out for the last half hour. You people want to talk. *(Tony exits.)*

HANK. Is it predicted at the Trinity site?

PETER. Yes. Rain, hail, lightning. It's moving through fast but it looks bad.

HANK. Goddamn.

IRENE. Yes, I'm sure He is damning us all.

HANK. They need water so badly here, but not tonight, guys.

PETER. It's moving fast, it'll probably clear by four or five.

IRENE. Oppie is calling it "Trinity"?

PETER. Yes.

IRENE. What is that? Father, Son and Holy Spirit?

PETER. I wouldn't presume to guess what he's thinking. You know Oppie, it's probably from some Latin poem, or Sanskrit, John

Donne. The ground at the site is covered with miles of electric cables, going everywhere. You just need one connection to short out to wreck everything. The detonator is electrical, lightning all around, we have no idea if it could be set off accidentally. By now the gadget's in place on the tower. Might as well be a lightning rod.

HANK. The gadget's up on a tower?

PETER. Yes. You knew that. *(Always the professor.)* What is the optimum height for an explosion? Ergo, how high is the tower?

HANK. *(After a moment.)* A hundred feet high.

PETER. Fermi has a new experiment. You know he's hands-on everything. He has little pieces of paper to drop before the test and during the test, to measure the displacement the shock wave causes. How far the blast wave blows his little scraps of paper. He's worked out a table — two meters equals so many thousand tons of TNT, three meters equals so much.

HANK. I love it. And I bet he's right on the money.

PETER. This, however, is not so lovely. This morning he says, very quietly to me, "In the event this gadget does not go off — with all these fission products we're creating, which would be the most effective poisoning agent, if we were to introduce it into the enemy's water supply?" I suppose so our experiments shouldn't be a complete waste. This is the way moral men are thinking now.

HANK. What did you say?

PETER. I said I'd think about it and tell him tomorrow. I'm sure he knows perfectly well.

IRENE. And what is? The most effective —

HANK. Probably strontium. *(Stron-tea-um.)*

PETER. Possibly strontium 90. Goes directly into the bone, replaces the calcium, and cannot be reversed. Essentially it would burn you to death from the inside out. Or at the very least induce leukemia. That should make everybody happy.

HANK. Jesus God.

IRENE. You want another?

PETER. No, one's my limit. But maybe we'll ask the Cantina to get bigger glasses.

HANK. This is always so good. I've never had this kind of tea before. Well, we don't drink tea. I guess it's too English. In the summer, iced tea. The folks haven't gone so far as to accept American food. Mom's terrified of anything in a can. She's like you like that; and that's the only way she's like you, believe me. Putting things up all summer. The basement's full of jars of — you know, they grow everything, or some neighbor does. Or they buy bushels of peaches at a time. Pasta and gravy, veal chops, that's the standbys. Not much meat since the war, just pasta now. They still find the cheese, God knows where. Tomatoes are American. They're from the New World. You wonder what the Italians did before Columbus. Imagine Italy without tomato sauce. Cream and cheese, I guess. Garlic. Coffee — is coffee American? Mom says that's all they drink in Italy now. Well, not now, I guess. This is wonderful; what is it?

PETER. It's just plain green tea, Hank, nothing extraordinary.

HANK. Do you get it from the pueblo?

PETER. They don't grow tea in New Mexico.

IRENE. It comes from China.

PETER. They have it at the commissary. And coffee comes from Africa.

HANK. I know nothing about food. You'd never guess, huh? China. Boy. The world. And haven't we made a mess of it.

IRENE. Italy. Ernesto Sanchez fell in Italy. A beautiful boy. He helped Peter dig the well.

HANK. I know. I mean I didn't know him. I know his dad. *(Tony enters.)*

IRENE. Good, I was hoping you'd come back.

TONY. Starting to smell like rain.

IRENE. We were talking about Ernesto. He was the first boy off the reservation to enlist.

TONY. Now they're all gone.

PETER. You wonder if any of them will come back.

IRENE. Peter.

PETER. I meant if they'll come back to the pueblo. When they come back, will they come back here?

TONY. And what they'll be. I think if they do, they're going to be as confused as I was. It's very different in the outside world.

HANK. And combat.

TONY. No, it's their land, not yours. They've been taught to defend it since they were children.

IRENE. What do you mean, it's the same old arguments up at the lodge?

PETER. Oh, they're having a merry old time — suffering our conscience. I think Bethe and Teller are not lifelong friends anymore. Bethe still insists Oppie could persuade the government to invite the Japanese to witness a demonstration of our progress. One week postponement. He's still saying that.

TONY. Forgetting the boys who are dying in the Pacific.

PETER. And Teller is saying, it's a little late for your reservations and invitations to the dance.

HANK. Bethe's right.

PETER. Yes, we're probably missing an important opportunity. Don't worry about it, Tony, it won't happen. Stimson has said no, Truman has said no, I don't think they'll pay much attention to a scientist.

HANK. "Engineer."

PETER. "Engineer." Teller said you're dreaming, and Hans said yes I am, terrible dreams.

IRENE. We all are.

PETER. With it getting so close, some people's nerves are failing. I'm not sure mine aren't also. I like this — Teller said: "I cannot understand, how you would want to tease this genie from his bottle with a string tied to his toe."

HANK. I can't think about Teller.

PETER. You didn't hear any of that, Tony.

TONY. I got this thing with my ears tonight.

PETER. Teller really is turning into a warmongering pig. Five years ago he was working underground, if you can believe it, fighting for the resistance. Bethe also thinks it's a tragic mistake not to have Russian scientists here, working with us.

HANK. Why not? After the war we'll all be sitting down at the table together, anyway.

PETER. Now who's dreaming.

HANK. The only way to develop peacetime applications of this … is for all the governments and scientists to work this out cooperatively.

PETER. — If they didn't listen to Einstein, they're not going to listen to us.

HANK. Anything else is unimaginable. Well, no, you can imagine it very easily, but who could live a decent life under the weight of this thing if all governments aren't working together?

PETER. I've given up on governments. I will be happy watering my zucchinis, thank you. Governments don't enjoy advocating a decent life, they like to say sacrifice and look to the future. For your children, right? And your children's children. And speaking of children, Oppie has come from advising the army on which Japanese city would best benefit from our work here.

HANK. Oh Christ, you might have known they'd form a target committee.

PETER. I'm sure they had many difficult considerations.

TONY. Guys.

PETER. Tony, I know perfectly well the MP's have been briefed enough to know we're making an explosive device.

TONY. And to say and hear nothing about it.

HANK. They'll have to find some place not already damaged too badly.

PETER. Otherwise how could they properly judge the destruction?

HANK. Preferably a town where there are some armament factories.

PETER. They'll need an excuse for blowing the place to hell.

HANK. Wooden houses.

PETER. No place where there are American prisoners held.

HANK. Right.

PETER. And not Kyoto. Too important artistically and historically.

HANK. They were pissed off enough about Dresden.

IRENE. Would you please not.

TONY. It's a shock for an Indian man to sit in a room with that talk.

HANK. Tony, we're all just —

IRENE. — It's just we're all so on edge, Tony —

HANK. No, don't make excuses for us, we're obscene.

PETER. The Indian just believes in a very different way of —

HANK. — There's no word in the Indian's language for what he believes in. There's no word for "religion," or "belief," or "dogma"

TONY. Oh, Christ.

HANK. Tony, just — [keep out of it.] Mrs. Martinez says the Indian's primary tenet is his trusteeship of nature — and here we are.

TONY. Maria Martinez has never heard the word "trusteeship" in her life.

HANK. Well, she said — words to that effect. It's just to know that for the Indian everything is just a part of life. Their art, their dance, the air, the rain, their work, their meals —

TONY. You're worse than the damn women from the museums; come around here and lecture on the Indian pottery. "Notice the graceful abstraction of the squash blossom here." The Indian can't listen to them, they have to walk off and puke.

IRENE. Or more likely go up in the mountains to get away from all our, I don't know. On solitary vigils. Fasting.

HANK. That sounds like you.

IRENE. No, I definitely stop short of fasting.

HANK. Rocks, rain, people, plants, the stars — All one thing.

And the thing is, they are. They're just different configurations of atoms. Tony, for a physicist to learn that the Indians have known that —

PETER. — If I know nothing else I know that one of the glories for me of our time here, is going to be remembering Hank explaining the Indian's philosophy to an Indian.

HANK. Well, excuse me for being spiritually stunned.

PETER. I really do have to shower. I'll be quick. Bainbridge said to bring a coat, it gets cold at night in the desert. *(Peter exits.)*

HANK. Does it really work? The smudge?

TONY. Yeah.

HANK. I thought you didn't believe in that stuff.

TONY. I never said that.

HANK. Man, it must have been so different for you, going to Europe, right off the reservation. I can't imagine. All you guys in Paris and Rome? It must have astonished you. And you them, probably. What was it like? Over there.

IRENE. I can't imagine either. Tell him about Josephine Baker.

HANK. Where the hell is Ryan?

TONY. I'll tell you about a fight I had in Denver once.

HANK. I know. You won and you got the scar on your leg.

TONY. And I was the one who spent the night in jail.

IRENE. Of course.

HANK. What was it like in Paris?

TONY. I was a kid, for crying out loud. I was eighteen. I mean I looked twenty-five or thirty but I didn't know nothing. I don't think the manager knew how young we were. It was profane, what we did. We were very damn good, I'll say that. We were the best in the country.

IRENE. He said modestly.

TONY. Well, we were, I'm sorry. The costumes, my God: full headdresses, turkey feathers, dyed cobalt blue, thirty ermine tails done up in my braids. These bibs, all beaded, front and back, over our privates.

IRENE. Not so private if I understand.

TONY. Just, now … [Let me tell it, please.] The manager in Paris had us naked.

IRENE. He's not lying.

TONY. Like showgirls. Well, that's what we were. That's what they expected. American savages, right? Four of us were completely naked. Under our whatever they call them.

IRENE. I liked "bibs."

HANK. Wasn't that awfully risqué back then?

TONY. Hell, it'd be risqué now. You'd never catch us trying something like that over here. They'd have our bare butts in jail. But all of Europe in 1924, '25, you wouldn't have believed it. We were a complete desecration of everything the Indian — lives. And we loved it, the women died for us. Especially Pauli. And me. I was gorgeous.

HANK. But not modest.

TONY. Not a bit of it. I looked almost more Anglo than Indian though. Too bad. But a washboard stomach. You could have washed your socks on my stomach. One woman did, her underpants. And as soon as we got away from the pueblo, we did the Harvest Dance. Big billboards all over Paris, "The Forbidden Harvest Dance. *La danse defendue de la moisson.* Never before seen by the white race." Totally sacrilegious. What did we care, we were kids. Riding on great ships, trains. I'd seen the train go by three times a week since I was born and never been on one before. Everything was paid for. Making what we thought was a fortune. Stage show entertainers; colored lights. Everyone stared on the street, everywhere we went. Asking for our autographs. I think they were disappointed we could write our names out. They wanted us to draw hieroglyphics. Well, Pauli couldn't. A real savage. And he looked it, too, completely Indian, nose like a hatchet, but a beautiful man. Women were mad for him. Well, I say man, he was, I guess, seventeen when we went over. Both of us exactly the same size, same build. The Bull dance — at the end, just Pauli and me back and forth with everyone else standing back, doubling up on the drums, very loud, over and over, just one rhythm, repeated for almost twenty minutes. Just the two of us, fighting it out.

HANK. I've seen that one.

TONY. Not the way we did it.

HANK. Well, not naked, but it was pretty steamy.

TONY. They can't do it now, they're a joke. We snorted and sweated and yelled like hyenas. Women fainted. Well, it was the thing to do back then. Paris, and Munich, Amsterdam, Berlin, Sweden, Norway, Denmark. Lord did they love us in Denmark, and did we love them. Blondes. Everywhere. We had our pictures taken. And movie pictures; bah! We were in the newsreels. Terrible business. I don't like to remember all the things we did.

HANK. No, come on, you were news. What would you expect?

TONY. The dances are not for show.

IRENE. The dances are prayers.

HANK. I know.

TONY. They're not to be taken photographs of. Or to show little glimpses of your privates and make the girls hot for you and the men angry and frightened. They're sacred. We didn't use eagle feathers, that would have been too real. But we put on a show for them.

HANK. How long were you over there?

TONY. Four years. Not all of us. We went over with twelve, four came back right away, couldn't take it. Two others came over to join us. When we came back, there were — seven. That last year we only worked maybe once every two weeks. We laid around, went to restaurants, outdoor cafes, wined and dined. Dressed in suits, hard shoes. Talked about world events, read the international papers. We thought we were something.

HANK. But you came back.

TONY. A complete drunk. Total alcoholic. I lived in New York, I lived in Chicago, Denver. I came back. No, I wouldn't have made a good chief.

HANK. Not after that.

TONY. They'd heard what we did. They could smell all those European women on us. And wine. And absinthe.

HANK. No. Really?

TONY. Oh, all of it. It had been illegal in France for years but it was everywhere.

HANK. What does it taste like?

TONY. Sweet licorice. On fire.

HANK. I imagined something completely different. Herbal or something.

TONY. You know what they found most fascinating about us? Tobacco. We were the Wild Red Men who had given the world tobacco. Everywhere we went people were poking tobacco at us like we couldn't exist without it; fish out of water. And you know what? Not one of us smoked. Indians don't smoke the way white people smoke. But we learned. What whores. We were fish out of water.

HANK. I'm surprised they believed in you. I mean people as sophisticated as the French are supposed to be.

TONY. You know why they believed in us? The first night in Paris they didn't know what to think. We did the first dance, they stared with their mouths open. We came off, the manager said, "I can see your white underpants, they think you're a fraud." We stripped. Didn't think a thing about it. The last dance we did was the Rain

26

Dance, we chanted for twenty minutes, the rhythm is hypnotic.

HANK. I've seen that one too, it is.

TONY. Then we, you know how slow it is, over and over, almost half an hour. We ended the dance — you know it just stops.

HANK. I know.

TONY. There's no climax to an Indian dance, it goes on and on and then it's over. We finished the show, came off. No applause. The audience sat there. We found out later they were completely exhausted — but they also were wondering what the hell they had seen with this Rain Dance. Curtain comes down, we go to our dressing rooms, the audience gets up and files out — they didn't even talk among themselves. They just went out into the streets. And it was pouring rain!

HANK. No. Perfect.

TONY. Floods all over France for a week. And we were famous!

IRENE. You didn't say there had been a drought.

TONY. There had been a drought. Five months. We didn't even know. Headline in the newspapers: AMERICAN RED MEN MAKE RAIN IN FRANCE!

IRENE. That's wonderful.

HANK. And they really thought you made it rain. With your dance.

TONY. *(Pause.)* If our hearts are right. When we dance. The rain will come.

IRENE. It's really looking threatening. I think your dance is working.

HANK. My God. You don't happen to know a —

TONY. — A dance to make it stop? No. Sorry, guy.

HANK. Look at that sky. Any other time. *(Hank moves outside. From off.)* It's actually beautiful, if you can discount the fact that it'll …

TONY. You weren't home last night. Or the night before.

IRENE. Did you come by too? I had to get away for a while.

TONY. I know.

IRENE. I should have said something.

TONY. No, that's okay. *(Tony and Irene move together and kiss like old lovers.)* You're probably going to be too nervous about Peter and them to get together tonight.

IRENE. I also might welcome the distraction …

TONY. Oh, I don't think I much like being thought of as a distraction.

IRENE. I wouldn't either.

TONY. Maybe we can drive up into the hills.

IRENE. What's the general direction of this…?

TONY. South. A place called the "Jornada del Muerto."

IRENE. "Journey of Death."

TONY. "Death March."

IRENE. Lordy, lordy.

HANK. *(Offstage.)* Did you see Ryan?

PETER. *(Offstage.)* No sign of him.

IRENE. You want a root beer?

TONY. You always have the best ideas.

PETER. *(Entering.)* It really does look like it could rain like one of those vulgar expressions.

HANK. *(Entering behind Peter.)* Everyone's leaving, most of the cars have pulled out. Dammit, where's Ryan? Goddamn.

PETER. Actually, the good money is betting that our little experiment will fail.

HANK. That would be just as satisfactory as far as I'm concerned.

PETER. Oh, definitely.

TONY. Why's that?

PETER. I came here primarily to prove what we wanted to do couldn't be done. Why, Tony? Because if we can't do it, they can't do it.

TONY. There are twenty-two boys from San Ildefonso in the Pacific.

IRENE. I know.

TONY. Miguel Sanchez got wounded. Not seriously.

IRENE. Maria told me.

TONY. I said where was he wounded? I meant in the head, in the leg, they said, "In the Pacific." At least he'll be coming home.

PETER. Twenty-two from San Ildefonso. I heard there are over a hundred from the Navaho reservation.

TONY. The Navaho breed like flies.

IRENE. Tony.

TONY. The only tribe since the white race came here that has increased instead of decreased.

HANK. Is that true?

TONY. Cockroaches. At least they're making themselves useful. You want to know a military secret? Maybe I shouldn't tell you.

HANK. You know a military secret?

TONY. Oh, yes. Can you keep a secret? I guess you can.

IRENE. Until tonight.

HANK. I think so.

TONY. Diego got back last month, he saw this over there. The Japs

28

have been breaking all our secret codes. Nobody knew how the devils did it. Diego says they could change codes twice a day, it didn't matter. Our boys got these clumsy decoding machines, takes about half an hour to read your own message. Japs had them decoded almost before we did. You know what code they devised? The Japs can't break it to save their lives.

HANK. No.

TONY. This is secret. I'm not lying.

IRENE. Trust us.

TONY. De-nay.

HANK. No.

IRENE. The language of the Navaho?

TONY. Yes. They've worked out some code. Horse means Jeep, mule means truck. That sort of thing.

IRENE. Oh, that's wonderful.

TONY. It is. That's why they got over three hundred Navaho boys over there. One traveling with every company. Diego says they just talk to each other on the phone, so there's no decoding time.

HANK. I love it.

TONY. They call themselves the Code Talkers.

PETER. That's beautiful.

TONY. Every one of 'em got his own bodyguard; guy's only job is to protect his Code Talker.

IRENE. Oh Tony ...

PETER. There was something like that in Kaiser Wilhelm the First's day. Messengers memorized messages, some pages long, and they all traveled with a bodyguard. Or the messenger thought he had a bodyguard. Actually the man guarding him went along so if they were captured, the bodyguard would kill the messenger.

TONY. *(Brief pause.)* My God. You travel all over Europe, you think you know the world; pretty sophisticated, I'd lay odds you're right.

PETER. I'd bet on it.

TONY. Even with the Code Talkers saving the army's ass over there, Diego says the troops got no respect for them. Won't eat their meals at the same table.

HANK. Let's just hope they take care of themselves. Or each other. I don't know why we still think of Europe as sophisticated. And we do. Even with all this — France folding like a fan — Hitler expunging the Jews, attacking all the — well, hell, you were there — you must have seen it in Munich.

PETER. The amazing thing to me. The what? The phenomenon was not Hitler, I was personally immune to Hitler, he looked like a foolish chimpanzee to me, but — Oh! My! The effect he had on even the most intelligent people — he was their savior, redeemer from this great distress and humiliation of losing a war, a nation physically bankrupt, in the middle of the Depression, with worthless money. And he said, Hitler said, "That you have found me among so many millions is the miracle of our time! And that I have found you. How deeply we feel in this hour the miracle that has brought us together!" And to stand beside friends, professors, your comrades at the laboratory, standing in a crowd listening to this monkey and feel beside you their chests heaving with emotion, their arms raising over their heads involuntarily, it was like a revival, it was evangelical. It built up gradually — from month to month until they mesmerized — beyond love and adoration, they believed in him. And he caused them to believe in themselves again. To see how he changed the way they saw themselves, prided themselves and began to distrust anyone who didn't believe. And how he grew because of them. Each feeding or building on the other, but you had to stand in the middle of this throng and see it happening to know, to understand, to believe it. It was amazing, messianic. It was — terrible. Amazing.

IRENE. And Peter turned to me and said, we are getting the hell out of here.

HANK. That's where I should have been. Over there. Everyone else my age …

IRENE. No. You belong here.

HANK. You still feel it. The obligation.

PETER. You belong here.

HANK. I wasn't even that damn important to this thing.

PETER. The first week we were here.

HANK. It just came to me.

PETER. That's the way inspiration works.

HANK. You're a great help. You guys. I'm getting so used to so many of the "engineers" having some kind of European accent, I think I'm getting one myself. From Munich to the middle of New Mexico? Practically in the desert? Whatever possessed you?

PETER. Believe me, we didn't even know how ridiculous we looked. And now you'd need explosives to get me out. Irene possessed me. What possessed you, darling?

IRENE. The desert.

HANK. I never know what you're thinking, Mrs. Snyders. You

30

NEW PLAYS

★ **INTIMATE APPAREL by Lynn Nottage.** The moving and lyrical story of a turn-of-the-century black seamstress whose gifted hands and sewing machine are the tools she uses to fashion her dreams from the whole cloth of her life's experiences. "...Nottage's play has a delicacy and eloquence that seem absolutely right for the time she is depicting..." –*NY Daily News*. "...thoughtful, affecting...The play offers poignant commentary on an era when the cut and color of one's dress—and of course, skin—determined whom one could and could not marry, sleep with, even talk to in public." –*Variety*. [2M, 4W] ISBN: 0-8222-2009-1

★ **BROOKLYN BOY by Donald Margulies.** A witty and insightful look at what happens to a writer when his novel hits the bestseller list. "The characters are beautifully drawn, the dialogue sparkles..." –*nytheatre.com*. "Few playwrights have the mastery to smartly investigate so much through a laugh-out-loud comedy that combines the vintage subject matter of successful writer-returning-to-ethnic-roots with the familiar mid-life crisis." –*Show Business Weekly*. [4M, 3W] ISBN: 0-8222-2074-1

★ **CROWNS by Regina Taylor.** Hats become a springboard for an exploration of black history and identity in this celebratory musical play. "Taylor pulls off a Hat Trick: She scores thrice, turning CROWNS into an artful amalgamation of oral history, fashion show, and musical theater..." –*TheatreMania.com*. "...wholly theatrical...Ms. Taylor has created a show that seems to arise out of spontaneous combustion, as if a bevy of department-store customers simultaneously decided to stage a revival meeting in the changing room." –*NY Times*. [1M, 6W (2 musicians)] ISBN: 0-8222-1963-8

★ **EXITS AND ENTRANCES by Athol Fugard.** The story of a relationship between a young playwright on the threshold of his career and an aging actor who has reached the end of his. "[Fugard] can say more with a single line than most playwrights convey in an entire script...Paraphrasing the title, it's safe to say this drama, making its memorable entrance into our consciousness, is unlikely to exit as long as a theater exists for exceptional work." –*Variety*. "A thought-provoking, elegant and engrossing new play..." –*Hollywood Reporter*. [2M] ISBN: 0-8222-2041-5

★ **BUG by Tracy Letts.** A thriller featuring a pair of star-crossed lovers in an Oklahoma City motel facing a bug invasion, paranoia, conspiracy theories and twisted psychological motives. "...obscenely exciting...top-flight craftsmanship. Buckle up and brace yourself..." –*NY Times*. "...[a] thoroughly outrageous and thoroughly entertaining play...the possibility of enemies, real and imagined, to squash has never been more theatrical." –*A.P.* [3M, 2W] ISBN: 0-8222-2016-4

★ **THOM PAIN (BASED ON NOTHING) by Will Eno.** An ordinary man muses on childhood, yearning, disappointment and loss, as he draws the audience into his last-ditch plea for empathy and enlightenment. "It's one of those treasured nights in the theater—treasured nights anywhere, for that matter—that can leave you both breathless with exhilaration and...in a puddle of tears." –*NY Times*. "Eno's words...are familiar, but proffered in a way that is constantly contradictory to our expectations. Beckett is certainly among his literary ancestors." –*nytheatre.com*. [1M] ISBN: 0-8222-2076-8

★ **THE LONG CHRISTMAS RIDE HOME by Paula Vogel.** Past, present and future collide on a snowy Christmas Eve for a troubled family of five. "...[a] lovely and hauntingly original family drama...a work that breathes so much life into the theater." –*Time Out*. "...[a] delicate visual feast..." –*NY Times*. "...brutal and lovely...the overall effect is magical." –*NY Newsday*. [3M, 3W] ISBN: 0-8222-2003-2

DRAMATISTS PLAY SERVICE, INC.
440 Park Avenue South, New York, NY 10016 212-683-8960 Fax 212-213-1539
postmaster@dramatists.com   www.dramatists.com

IRENE. I had a nervous breakdown, Hank. As we were leaving Germany. It got worse in London and then New York. The doctor there said I should go away for a while, maybe even a year. Some friend of — do you remember?

PETER. I've always laid the blame on some sadistic acquaintance of Szilard's. *(zil-LARD'S.)*

IRENE. Someone said we might go to the desert. It sounded fine.

PETER. Any place to get away.

IRENE. Serendipity. Good fortune when you're not looking for it.

HANK. I'm glad you decided to stay.

IRENE. There was no "deciding" about it. I couldn't have left if I wanted to. *(Pause.)* I'll tell you something if you stop looking at your watch. The first time I met Oppenheimer he was on a pack trip. He and his brother have owned a place north of here for years; they used to go camping and tramping around this area. He came to the house one morning asking for Peter. He's so thin and such a cowboy, such a "dude." The energy field he had around him, the focus, the intensity, the way he looked around, just being around him was exhausting. We don't get people like that around here. You knew he wasn't missing a thing. He knew the hills were sacred to the Indians. He said he thought there was a stronger spiritual pull here than any place he'd ever known.

HANK. We've talked about that.

IRENE. He didn't tell me, but when he came that day, the minute he hit the door, fanning himself with that big old hat, I knew he had come to take it all away. All the peace, all the spirituality he admired so much. And so did he. He spoke about the place with such — regret. He stopped at the door when he was leaving, and turned around, he was so thin, and said, "You may want to join us — in spite of the lovely place you have here."

HANK. The man has no ego at all.

IRENE. Oh, don't be absurd, he's a man, isn't he? You don't know what earthly good they are until they're all gone. Has no ego? I think he and Teller are two of the most arrogant men I've ever known. But what I was trying to say, Hank — when the war broke out, like you, I felt it was selfish of me to stay home. I should get a war job like all the other women. Be a Rosie the Riveter. I know what you mean by "you feel the force of obligation." But for some reason I knew I was supposed to stay.

HANK. Then Oppie said Peter would need a draftsman. And you found your war job.

IRENE. I wasn't just living with a brilliant physicist in the middle of the desert by chance. You're still looking at your watch.

HANK. I'm sorry. *(A loud thunder clap.)* Wow. Listen to that. It won't matter a damn to them, they'll go right on with it.

PETER. They have to.

HANK. Peter, we were in a race with Germany! Why else did you come here? But Germany's defeated, it's gone.

TONY. There are still twenty-two boys from the reservation fighting in the Pacific.

HANK. I know. You said. And three hundred Navaho telegraphing De-nay around the Pacific Islands.

TONY. Don't the Japs have scientists too?

HANK. You kidding? Some of the best. Hagiwara. *(Ha-gee-wahr-ah.)* Nishina. *(Nye-sheen-ah.)* What they probably don't have, they don't have the money, Tony.

TONY. Good.

HANK. You can't imagine how much money we've spent. It's a golden project, a blank check. We're getting shipments from factories and refineries from all over the country.

TONY. Good.

HANK. This has cost billions. This — this — night. This night. *(Hank pushes over the table. Everything goes everywhere.)* I should go.

TONY. And do what? Stand outside in the dark?

HANK. I have to get my coat.

PETER. We'll pick it up on the way.

HANK. I've come to the most peaceful place on earth, only to turn it inside out. We all have. As you said. Knowing all the while what we were doing … Fawning over the Indians and their sacred shrines and their old customs and sacred lands, desecrating everything we touched. I have a piece of Maria's. I talked with her all one afternoon. I think she's the most unassuming person I've ever met. Some dealer was there. She said, "Maria, you're signing pieces that you don't make. They're not the quality of your work. You can't sign pieces you don't make yourself." And Maria said, "The girls get more money from their pieces if I sign them." Imagine any other artist signing work less good than his own. Well, actually, you would, probably. I said I wanted to buy something. I was looking at what she had laid out on the blanket, spread out on the table. After the dealer left Maria went in back and brought out this huge, beautiful bowl, it must be nearly a foot across. It's the only thing I've ever bought that was beautiful. I'll walk back to the Bronx to keep from breaking it. It's this place. She

33

told me … Well, she knew I was your friend. She said having been adopted by the tribe you'd be buried as the Indians are — with no marker on your grave. The only marker —

IRENE. Hank.

HANK. Just a few pieces of broken pottery on your grave. She showed me the pieces she'd made to be — I'm sorry. They're beautiful. Jesus, what kind of life am I living? The world is over. I hope they've enjoyed it. Everything that's gone before tonight is broken, extinct, gone, evaporated, useless. If the world doesn't end tonight, it ends anyway.

IRENE. Hank, I didn't need them all laughing and joking up at the lodge, I don't need that either.

HANK. I know.

TONY. The world will end tonight?

PETER. Early tomorrow morning.

IRENE. At four o'clock.

HANK. What?

IRENE. You said six hours.

HANK. No. Better mathematicians than I have assured us it won't.

PETER. So they tell us. Well, no, actually I worked it out for myself and it won't.

HANK. You did? So did I.

PETER. I imagine, secretly, we all did.

TONY. Okay.

HANK. Yeah, I know. On paper the world won't end tonight. They're going to take it away from us, Peter. The government. We're going to have no say at all in the development of this — energy. Well, the only say we'll have is if we want to continue to be a part of it. *(There is a car horn heard from outside. Tony goes to the door.)*

PETER. You've always known that.

HANK. No, I did not. I didn't know that. I was much more naive than that.

TONY. Does Ryan have a tan Chivvy?

HANK. Yeah. Well. *(Pause.)* Szilard talked to President Truman last month. God, it's the same over and over again. He took Truman a letter from Einstein of all people. They're being ignored completely, condescended to like children.

PETER. I signed the petition same as you.

HANK. Peter, the American government is notoriously bone-headed when it comes to science. They just use us. They're doing it again. They never listen. Shamed, and banished — ignored, and

asked to do more.

PETER. Henry, think. Nobel thought he had ended the possibility of all future wars with the discovery of dynamite.

HANK. — I know, and so does Oppenheimer, he's said it a dozen times. It's not that. Teller has asked me to stay on. They've offered me a five-year contract. About six times any human salary.

IRENE. I thought we were nearly finished.

HANK. With science, you're never finished. Bigger and better mousetraps. Teller doesn't give a damn about the "gadget" except that he needs it to ignite his "super" bomb. Sorry, Tony, bomb bomb bomb. He said the government has given approval. To work on that and to simplify the gadget and find a way to mass-produce it. To build an arsenal.

PETER. Oh dear God.

HANK. It isn't just this one time tonight. I love it here so much.

IRENE. Peter?

PETER. Believe me, we won't stay. We're all done.

HANK. I don't know how I can go back, leave this place.

IRENE. We'll understand if you stay. *(Car horn.)*

PETER. We have to go. We won't be needed here much longer. We'll be going home. Tony isn't working tonight. You should probably be with him.

IRENE. I will.

TONY. Could I ask you guys a question? About this work? —

HANK. Tony …

PETER. Yes, why not.

HANK. Whatever your question is — I can't believe it will ever happen. They'll never use this.

PETER. Hank, don't fool yourself.

TONY. Irene said two trucks left here early Friday morning. One truck went to Ground Zero — and the other truck kept right on going. By now your gadget is on a plane on a runway in San Francisco — ready to be carried to the middle of the Pacific. And there's a B-29 bomber on an island in the middle of the Pacific — ready to take your gadget to Japan. As soon as they get a phone call from Ground Zero tonight.

HANK. *(To Peter.)* Is that true?

PETER. I don't know. I would hope not.

HANK. You couldn't possibly know something like that.

TONY. I thought you believed the Indians knew everything. Can it really do it? One bomb? Is going to end the war? We'll have peace?

HANK. If the test is successful, the war will be over in a month.

PETER. Less.

TONY. Thank God. Man, you guys …

IRENE. Only that wasn't what he asked, was it?

PETER. We really have to leave now.

HANK. I know. You go on, Peter.

PETER. You're not going? To the test?

HANK. I'm not going, no.

PETER. Are you sure?

HANK. For my children? And my children's children?

PETER. I wouldn't miss it for the world. It's starting to rain. *(Peter exits.)*

HANK. Good — they need it here.

IRENE. Are you going to be all right?

HANK. Yeah. I have to pack. Dig up the bus schedule. See how soon I can leave here.

TONY. We'll see you tomorrow.

HANK. Oh, yeah. *(Irene and Tony exit. After a moment, Hank slowly starts restoring order to the room. He picks up the smudge, lights it, and follows the Indian ritual of cleansing the room, gently waving the smudge into every quarter of the room. The herbal and pungent smell fill the theater. He puts the smudge down and leans against the table. Lights fade to black.)*

End of Play

PROPERTY LIST

Drinks
Glass of sherry (IRENE)
Smudge, match (HANK)

SOUND EFFECTS

Thunder
Car horn

draw and paint and nod and smile and listen and look off at some distant hill. I've known you over a year, and I learned tonight that you'd just been married when you came here. You never tell anyone anything about yourself. *(Pause. He looks at her, expecting something.)* Fine. To hell with it. It doesn't matter. Where the devil is he?

TONY. There's no need to be rude, Hank.

HANK. I'm sorry, forgive me. I can't —

PETER. You know he's not thinking right if he calls Irene Mrs. Snyders.

HANK. Did I? Sorry. It's a good German name.

PETER. Flemish.

HANK. Flemish?

TONY. Sit down. Drink a beer. Do something useful.

IRENE. *(After a pause.)* Serendipity.

TONY. Who's that one?

IRENE. Good luck. When you're not looking for it. I was looking for something a lot larger than luck. Salvation.

HANK. I hope you don't think you've told anybody anything. Maybe you should write your autobiography.

IRENE. A friend of ours said that. She thought — doesn't matter.

HANK. Do I know her?

IRENE. Her husband taught at the Los Alamos School. A government project kicked them out.

HANK. They must love us. Do you still see her?

IRENE. You don't move very far from here. They write.

HANK. Do they know about us?

IRENE. I don't imagine they care, Hank. This place is what they want to know about. How the spring planting went, was there a late frost, did the river leave its banks, was it too dry to plant, or one year, actually, too wet. How many jars of jelly, how many of relish. With the war, are there enough men left on the reservation to work the fields. And no, there's not, so how is everyone coping. They're people of the land.

HANK. And did you? Write your autobiography?

IRENE. We came here for quiet, why should I be the one who disturbs it. What's the point? "European physicist and his batty wife move to the American Southwest. Live among the Indians." I don't think so.

HANK. *(A pause.)* "Salvation"? *(Beat.)* I really do know why Oppie trusts you to work on the project. You tell no one anything. Not really. He must have seen it immediately.